Remembering
Raleigh

Dusty Wescott and Kenneth E. Peters

TURNER
PUBLISHING COMPANY

Two Raleigh trolley cars pass each other in this undated photograph.

Remembering
Raleigh

Turner Publishing Company
www.turnerpublishing.com

Remembering Raleigh

Library of Congress Control Number: 2010924247

ISBN: 978-1-59652-637-2

Printed in the United States of America

ISBN 978-1-68336-876-2 (pbk.)

CONTENTS

Created as the state's capital city in 1792, Raleigh was laid out according to a plan drawn up by state senator William Christmas. The plan included four main thoroughfares radiating outward from the central statehouse. The southern avenue—Fayetteville Street—became Raleigh's commercial district. This early photograph of Fayetteville Street, thought to be from the 1860s, shows E. Besson's Tailor Shop.

Acknowledgments

This volume, *Remembering Raleigh,* is the result of the cooperation and efforts of many individuals and organizations. It is with great thanks that we acknowledge in particular the valuable contribution of the North Carolina State Archives and the Library of Congress.

PREFACE

Raleigh has thousands of historic photographs that reside in archives, both locally and nationally. This book began with the observation that, while those photographs are of great interest to many, they are not easily accessible. During a time when Raleigh is looking ahead and evaluating its future course, many people are asking, How do we treat the past? These decisions affect every aspect of the city—architecture, public spaces, commerce, infrastructure—and these, in turn, affect the way that people live their lives. This book seeks to provide easy access to a valuable, objective look into the history of Raleigh.

The power of photographs is that they are less subjective than words in their treatment of history. Although the photographer can make subjective decisions regarding subject matter and how to capture and present it, photographs seldom interpret the past to the extent textual histories can. For this reason, photography is uniquely positioned to offer an original, untainted look at the past, allowing the viewer to learn for himself what the world was like a century or more ago.

This project represents countless hours of review and research. The researchers and writers have reviewed thousands of photographs in numerous archives. We greatly appreciate the generous assistance of those listed in the acknowledgments of this work, without whom this project could not have been completed.

The goal in publishing this work is to provide broader access to this set of extraordinary photographs which seek to inspire, provide perspective, and evoke insight that might assist people who are responsible for determining Raleigh's future. In addition, the book seeks to preserve the past with adequate respect and reverence.

With the exception of touching up imperfections that have accrued with the passage of time and cropping where necessary, no changes have been made. The focus and clarity of many images are limited to the technology and the ability of the photographer at the time they were recorded.

The work is divided into eras. Beginning with some of the earliest known photographs of Raleigh, the first section records photographs from the Civil War era through the late nineteenth century. The second section spans the early years of the twentieth century through World War I. Section Three moves to the twenties and thirties. The last section covers the World War II era up to recent times.

In each of these sections we have made an effort to capture various aspects of life through our selection of photographs. People, commerce, transportation, infrastructure, religious institutions, and educational institutions have been included to provide a broad perspective.

We encourage readers to reflect as they go walking in Raleigh, strolling through the city, its parks, and its neighborhoods. It is the publisher's hope that in utilizing this work, longtime residents will learn something new and that new residents will gain a perspective on where Raleigh has been, so that each can contribute to its future.

—*Todd Bottorff, Publisher*

The Raleigh and Gaston Railroad Office Building, circa 1870s. Constructed in Raleigh during the early 1860s to house offices for the first railroad to serve the capital city, this building was embellished with a wrought-iron front porch in the 1870s. Later known as the Seaboard Coast Line Building, after that railroad absorbed the Raleigh and Gaston line, the structure was moved in 1977 from its original location to its present home at 413 North Salisbury Street.

TALE OF A CITY

(1860s–1899)

A parade marches along Raleigh's Fayetteville Street, where paradegoers crowd the sidewalks and storefronts to watch the event.

This view of the North Carolina State Capitol was recorded in 1861 and shows Governor David Reid in the foreground. A graceful granite structure that was completed between 1833 and 1840, this statehouse was built to replace an earlier 1794 building that burned to the ground in June 1831.

A unit of the Raleigh Light Infantry lines up along Morgan Street just south of the North Carolina State Capitol, circa 1875.

A Raleigh landmark for more than 130 years, the Briggs Building opened in 1874 as a home for Thomas H. Briggs & Sons, a building supply and hardware business. The Briggs family did business on the first floor, renting out the upper floors to other retailers. After the family-owned hardware business moved to a suburban location in 1995, the building was sold and renovated for use by non-profit organizations.

Opened in 1850 on Raleigh's Fayetteville Street, the Yarborough House quickly became known as the city's finest hotel. Over the years it would host the likes of William Jennings Bryan, Andrew Johnson, William Howard Taft, Woodrow Wilson, and—at the height of the Civil War—Mrs. Jefferson Davis, First Lady of the Confederacy. The hotel fell victim to a destructive fire in July 1928 and was not rebuilt.

The simplest modes of transportation were sometimes relied on in nineteenth-century North Carolina. This image of the North Carolina State Capitol from circa the 1880s features an ox-drawn cart.

The 100-block of Fayetteville Street in Raleigh following the Great Blizzard of 1899. Striking the Eastern Seaboard in February, the storm brought record snowfall to cities from Georgia to New England. In Raleigh, 17.7 inches of snow fell, a record that stood until 1927.

Merchants along the 200 block of Fayetteville Street in Raleigh dig out from under the snow dumped during the Great Blizzard of 1899.

This Greek Revival–style mansion once graced Raleigh's Peace Street and served throughout much of the nineteenth century as one of the city's most prominent homes. Built in the 1840s by Nancy Lane Mordecai, the residence earned the name "Devereux House" when Mordecai's daughter Margaret married John Devereux and then lived here. The house was razed circa 1900 after the estate was subdivided into smaller lots.

In the late 1800s and early 1900s, several privately owned drugstores operated along a four-block stretch of Fayetteville Street in downtown Raleigh. One of the most popular of these establishments was Brantley's Drug Store. Located at the corner of Fayetteville and Hargett streets, it was popular both for its soda fountain and its medicinal potions.

Flooding of the Eno River in 1899 envelops Eno Station Mill.

Chartered in 1891, the Baptist Female University opened its first campus in a large Queen Anne–style structure at Edenton and Blount streets in Raleigh. The school quickly expanded, changing its name to Meredith College in 1909.

During the early 1900s Raleigh's main electric company, Carolina Power & Light, took a vast number of downtown images to archive their power line system. This CP&L photograph depicts Martin Street, looking west from Salisbury Street. In the distance, just to the right of center, can be seen the Raleigh Hotel and Nash Square.

Tobacco Trusts and Trolley Cars

(1900–1919)

"Aunt Betsy" was a popular postcard image from Raleigh in the early 1900s.

A Raleigh merchant poses on the east side of the 100 block of Fayetteville Street, circa 1910. In the background is the marquee for the Grand Theater, one of the city's earliest motion picture houses.

Workers pave East Lane Street in Raleigh during the summer of 1906. The wagon at far-left advertises Harley-Davidson motorcycles.

A circus parade—complete with elephants—turns the corner of Fayetteville and Morgan streets in Raleigh, circa 1900. Fayetteville Street served as the city's central parade route and celebration site until its conversion into a pedestrian mall in the late 1970s.

Before completion of the dam that created Falls Lake in 1981, the Falls of the Neuse River was a popular destination for picnickers. This extended family enjoys an outing at the Falls in 1902.

The northeast corner of Fayetteville and Martin streets in Raleigh housed the Citizens National Bank by 1914, when this photograph is believed to have been taken. Constructed a year earlier, the ten-story edifice was the city's tallest structure at the time.

In March 1919, the 200-block of Fayetteville Street in Raleigh is festooned with banners as a crowd awaits the beginning of a parade to honor the state's returning World War I veterans. The North Carolina State Capitol is visible at center in the background.

Raleigh premiered the state's first streetcar system on Christmas Day 1886. Originally powered by mules, the system was electrified in 1891. Called the Raleigh Street Railway, the operation would later fall under the ownership of the Carolina Power & Light Company. In this 1910 photograph, a Raleigh trolley car crosses Martin Street as it moves down tracks along Fayetteville Street.

By the 1900s football began to compete with baseball as the most popular spectator sport on America's college campuses. Despite being frowned upon by faculty (and parents) who found it too violent, college football grew in popularity during the 1920s and 1930s. This image depicts the North Carolina A&M College (now North Carolina State University) football squad from circa 1905 to 1910.

Constructed between 1874 and 1879 on the southwest corner of Fayetteville and Martin streets in Raleigh, the Century Post Office Building was the first federal structure erected in the South after the Civil War. The building continues to serve as a downtown post office today.

A horse-drawn buggy carrying William Henry Smith and Margaret Alice Baugh passes Union Square and the North Carolina Statehouse in Raleigh, circa 1908.

Chartered by the General Assembly in 1887, North Carolina A&M College (now known as North Carolina State University) first opened its doors to students in Raleigh on October 3, 1889. The first building constructed on the new campus was Holliday Hall, pictured here in 1909.

Built between 1892 and 1910, Pilot Mill was one of only a handful of textile mills located in Raleigh. Most North Carolina textile mills sponsored musical and athletic clubs for their employees to participate in. The Pilot Mill Cotton Band poses here for a portrait.

Experiments in steam, internal combustion, and electric powered vehicles were ongoing early in the new century. Running the streets of Raleigh in 1909, this utility truck advertises its reliance on electric power. By the 1930s, gasoline had become the fuel of choice in Raleigh and across the nation.

Work is in progress on the dome of the State Capitol here around 1909.

First hosting students in 1899, the Main Building of Raleigh's Baptist Female University (later Meredith College) was designed by A. G. Bauer. Its lower floors held classrooms and meeting spaces while the upper floors served as dormitories for both students and instructors. When Meredith moved to a new campus in West Raleigh in 1926, the building became the Mansion Park Hotel. It was demolished in 1967.

Raleigh has been the site for the North Carolina State Penitentiary since 1870, when construction began on this imposing Gothic structure. Known as "Central Prison," the building was designed by Ohio architect Levi Scofield. Taking 14 years to complete at a cost of $1.25 million, the structure housed the state's prison population until the 1980s, when a new facility was built to replace the aging edifice.

Facing east on Hillsborough Street in Raleigh toward the west front of the North Carolina State Capitol, in the year 1909. Prominent in the photograph is the Confederate Memorial, a monument honoring North Carolinians killed during the Civil War.

This rooftop image, probably taken from atop the former Commercial National Bank building in Raleigh, faces west down Martin Street from its intersection with Fayetteville Street, circa 1915. Standing prominently in the center of the image is the Tucker Building.

This panorama of downtown Raleigh, circa 1915, faces north toward the distant State Capitol, with Fayetteville Street to the left and Wilmington Street running up the right.

Horse-drawn delivery carts, such as this one (at far-left) for Henry G. DeBoy's Grocery Store at Fayetteville and Davie streets in Raleigh, were common at the turn of the century.

The Raleigh Banking & Trust Company was erected on the southwest corner of Fayetteville and Hargett streets in Raleigh in 1913. It replaced an 1868 structure that was affectionately known as the "Round Steps Bank" owing to its curved stairway. In 1928-30, the bank added an additional eight stories above the original three-story facility, creating an eleven-story skyscraper.

From the dome of the North Carolina State Capitol, a photographer captures Fayetteville Street in the mid-1910s. Visible here are the busy streetcar track running down the avenue, the Grand Theater marquee (left), and the Citizens National Bank building (left-center), then Raleigh's tallest structure.

The scene on a rainy-day, muddy Wilmington Street in Raleigh in 1915. World War I would delay the paving of this main artery downtown.

A line crew hoists a utility pole into position at West Martin and McDowell streets in 1916. Horse-power had by no means vanished as the new century got under way.

Fayetteville Street in downtown Raleigh, 1917.

Martin Street as it appeared in 1917, facing east from the intersection at McDowell Street. A portion of the Raleigh Hotel is visible at far-left, followed by the Strand Theater.

Another 1917 view of Martin Street, looking west from Wilmington Street toward Fayetteville Street, captures the Raleigh business district at night.

Linemen pose for a group shot with Carolina Power & Light's first two-ton utility truck in 1919, following the close of World War I. Some of these men were no doubt veterans of the recent worldwide conflict.

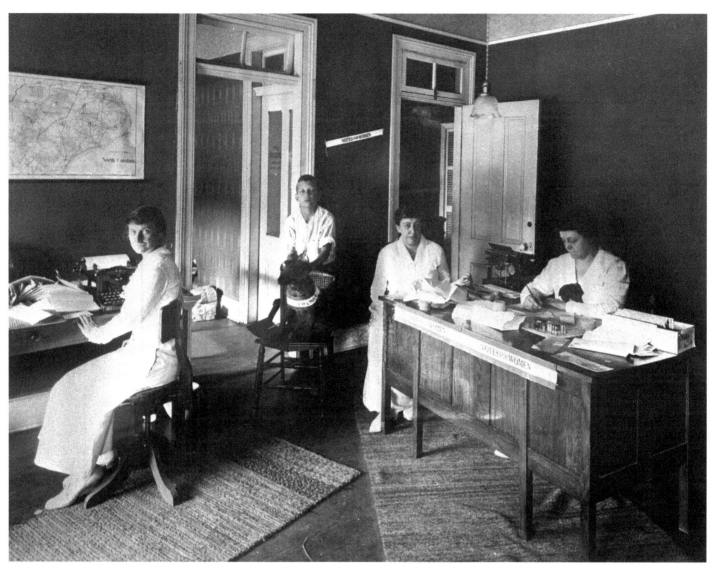

Suffragists at the Raleigh headquarters in 1920 pursue one of their goals: admittance at the ballot box for women.

A night view of Fayetteville Street, from the top of the North Carolina State Capitol, in 1924.

HAPPY DAYS ARE HERE . . . AND GONE

(1920–1939)

Andrew Johnson, 17th president of the United States, was born in Raleigh on December 29, 1808, inside this detached kitchen outbuilding on Fayetteville Street. The structure has been preserved and stands today in Raleigh's Mordecai Historic Park.

Several small, private airfields operated around Raleigh in the 1920s before a municipal site was dedicated. One of them, Marshburn-Robbins Airfield, was located along Old Garner Road south of the city. Pictured in 1927 are the Mills family and aviator Alton Stewart (fourth from the right), a Harnett County native.

Scene on the 100 block of
Fayetteville Street, circa 1920s.

Built in 1892 on Dawson Street west of Nash Square, Raleigh's Union Depot served railroad passengers until 1950. Parts of the structure are still in use today as offices.

The North Carolina A&M College (now North Carolina State University) football squad poses for a group shot in front of the grandstand at Riddick Field.

Here the football team at North Carolina A&M lines up for a practice drill.

This view from an upper window of the Masonic Temple Building at 133 Fayetteville Street shows the Raleigh Banking & Trust Building on the corner of Fayetteville and Hargett streets after its expansion from three to eleven stories in 1930.

Carolina Air Lines operated briefly during the 1920s out of Marshburn-Robbins Field south of Raleigh. This photograph depicts a young man in the cockpit of one of the company's Waco II airplanes.

These two Waco airplanes were delivered to the Curtis Travel Air Service in Raleigh in the late 1920s.

The Academy of Music Building (center, with "North Carolina Cotton Growers Co-operative" signage) was erected on the southwest corner of Salisbury and Martin streets in Raleigh in 1893. The structure served as a home for the finest theatrical productions in the city for two decades. Will Rogers, W. C. Fields, Ethel and John Barrymore, and other celebrated performers strode across its stage.

Opening on July 4, 1912, Bloomsbury Park was an early Raleigh amusement park at the end of the new Glenwood Avenue trolley line. Here, the Bloomsbury Park trolley travels alongside the route to the park.

A cold, wintry day on Fayetteville Street in 1923 finds the capital city astir with prosperity. The automobile has replaced the horse and buggy, and local merchants appear to be doing a brisk business.

The Confederate Soldiers Monument dominates the foreground in this view of Salisbury Street and the State Capitol in the mid-1920s. In memory of the thousands of North Carolinians who fought and died in the Civil War, the monument carries the legend "First at Bethel—Last at Appomattox."

The scene at Jones Street on a day in 1925. Traffic waits for the train to pass, idling behind the crossing bar, with the 1910 steam plant and streetcar garage in view beyond. Both buildings remain standing today.

The water-powered grist mill at Yates Pond, built around 1756, is seen here in the 1920s. Hurricane Fran would destroy the dam and waterwheel in 1996, but the historic mill, one of the last of its kind, would be restored to become a museum and park.

By the 1920s, East Hargett Street in Raleigh had become a thriving business district for the city's African-American community. The hotel sign in this image hung from the Lightner Arcade, a business enterprise opened by Calvin Lightner in 1924. The arcade provided offices for several black-owned businesses and operated a hotel for African-Americans.

The First Wake County Courthouse predated Raleigh by nearly 20 years. The Second Wake County Courthouse, opened in 1794 on the 300 block of Fayetteville Street, was the first to stand in the new capital city. It was succeeded in the 1830s by the Third Wake County Courthouse. The structure pictured here was the Fourth Wake County Courthouse, built in 1915. It stood until the 1960s, when it was replaced with the current county facility.

Angus W. McLean served as the governor of North Carolina from 1925 to 1929. A Robeson County native, he poses here with his wife in front of the Executive Mansion in Raleigh.

A Carolina Power & Light Company trolley car clanks along Hillsborough Street in West Raleigh, circa 1927. The still-incomplete North Carolina State University Bell Tower is just visible in the distance, on the left.

A crowd gathers at the corner of Fayetteville and Hargett streets outside the Raleigh Banking & Trust Company offices. Although it has been suggested that this image depicts a 1929 run on the bank, the behavior and attire of the crowd implies an event less onerous.

The North Carolina State Capitol at night.

The North Carolina Revenue Building at 2 South Salisbury Street in Raleigh, circa 1930.

When he died in 1839, Raleigh merchant John Rex left a legacy to the city—a bequest that could be used for the establishment of a hospital. His funds were not utilized until 1894, when St. John's Hospital on South Street was purchased and renamed Rex Hospital. It is seen here in the 1930s before the hospital moved to a larger location on St. Mary's Street.

The Hotel Carolina stood on the northeast corner of Hargett and Dawson streets in Raleigh for much of the twentieth century. This location, adjacent Nash Square, placed it within walking distance of the Union Passenger Railroad Station.

In view here are the reconstructed walls of Fort Raleigh at Manteo. In 1587 John White, appointed governor of the settlement, left for England to restock the colony's supplies. Political complications prevented his return until 1590, whereupon he found that all of the English colonists on the Roanoke Island settlement had vanished. Now known as "the Lost Colony," the settlement's disastrous fate is still a mystery.

When the Raleigh Civic Auditorium burned to the ground in 1930, the city wasted no time replacing it. Just two years later, Memorial Auditorium opened on South Street on the site of an early governor's mansion.

The Raleigh Municipal Building opened at 333 Fayetteville Street in 1911. When the adjacent auditorium complex burned in 1930, the structure was saved by firemen and continued on as City Hall for another 30 years.

North Carolina governor Clyde R. Hoey poses outside the State Capitol with several men and an S. H. Bacon Materials Company truck in 1939.

This aerial view shows the old Catholic Orphanage. Established in 1899 by Father Thomas F. Price, the complex stood in the Nazareth neighborhood south of present-day Western Boulevard. After its closing, part of the site was used by the Tammy Lynn Center in the early 1970s. By the late 1980s, much of the land had been purchased by North Carolina State University for its Centennial Campus.

Named for a Raleigh business leader who was also a strong advocate for public education, Needham Broughton High School opened in 1929 on St. Mary's Street. The school is now the oldest continuously operating public high school in Raleigh, with an enrollment of more than 2,100 students.

At least one of the snakes St. Patrick drove from Ireland seems to have landed in Raleigh. During St. Patrick's Brawl Parade, put on by North Carolina State College in 1932, it slithers through the crowd of onlookers.

Traffic is light at these Amoco and Esso service stations in 1935. Gasoline prices averaged 17 cents a gallon that year, but 17 cents was a lot of change in out-of-hope, Depression-era Raleigh.

A close-up look at this Amoco station reveals the whimsical architecture of stations built early in the automobile age. Its terra-cotta roofing, in particular, was an element common to many stations across the nation.

The Detective Division of the Raleigh Police Department stand for a formal portrait in 1938.

In view here is a Raleigh filling station and tire sales company.

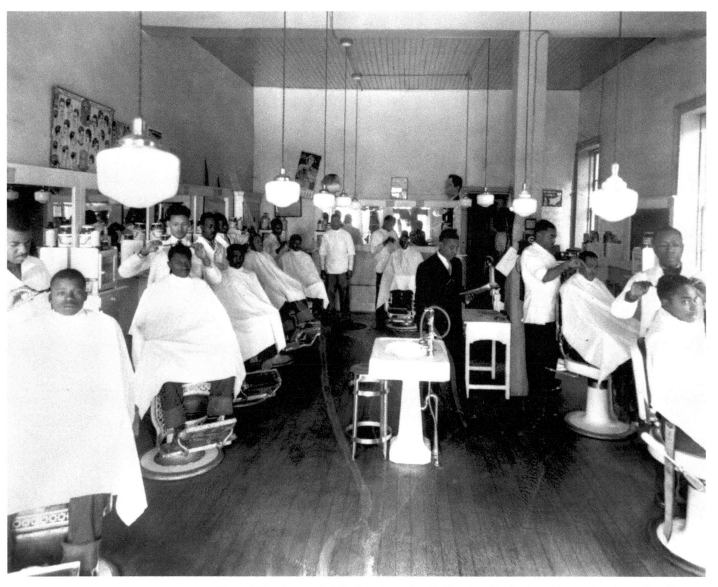

Samuel Harris founded the Harris Barber College in 1930 in the Lightner Arcade on East Hargett Street. Established to teach skills to African-American men, the college moved to its current location on South Blount Street in 1942. The Class of 1939 is depicted here.

By the 1920s, Fayetteville Street supported no fewer than seven drugstores along its four main blocks. One of the most popular was the Boon-Iseley Drug Store on the 100 block.

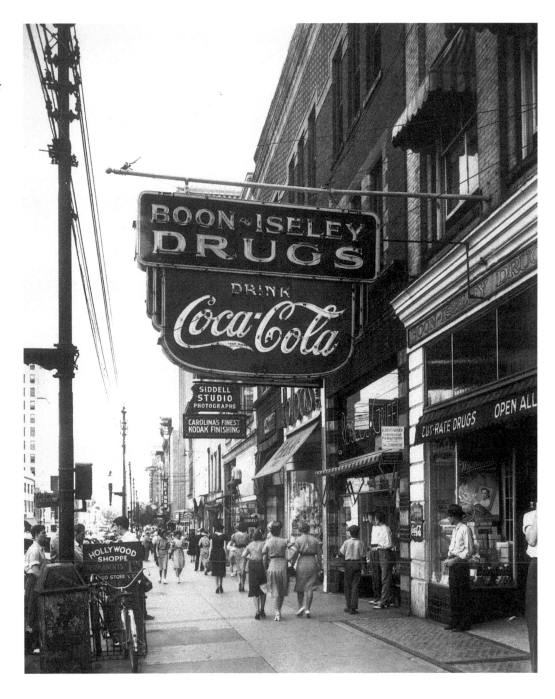

The Royal Theater, located on East Hargett Street, was one of two movie houses operated for black patrons during the first half of the twentieth century.

Fayetteville Street is festooned with Christmas decorations in this 1938 holiday photograph.

LET FREEDOM RING ALONG TOBACCO ROAD

(1940–1960s)

The State Capitol as it appeared in the early 1940s as North Carolina prepared for the war effort. Germany's U-boats threatened the coast, resources were being marshaled for the coming conflict, and the workforce was being retrained for service in the military in defense of the nation.

On May 20, 1940, a parade celebrates the centennial of the 1840 North Carolina State Capitol.

The intersection of Hargett and Salisbury streets in downtown Raleigh. Standing on the southeast corner is the eleven-story Odd Fellows Building, constructed in 1924.

A neon sign invites patrons into Blackwelders.

Created on land donated by Richard Stanhope Pullen in 1887, Pullen Park was North Carolina's first public park. In this photograph from January 28, 1940, ice skaters enjoy a winter afternoon on the park's Lake Howell.

Looking south at Fayetteville Street from the North Carolina State Capitol, 1941. The height of commercial and retail activity along Fayetteville Street took place in the 1940s preceding the development of the city's first suburban shopping center—Cameron Village—in 1949.

In 1941, a group of spectators downtown watches a spelling bee sponsored by radio station WRAL. Behind the proceedings, posters inside the display windows of McLellans advertise National Dairy Month, Your Hit Parade, and various products sold by the store.

Passengers board a city bus in 1941 at the intersection of Martin and Fayetteville streets. Motorized coaches had replaced the city's electric streetcars by 1933. Behind the Eckerd's sign, at center, is the 1874 Briggs Hardware Building.

Devereux Meadow Baseball Park was built in the late 1930s as a Works Progress Administration project. It was home to the Raleigh Capitals minor-league baseball team for many seasons. For some time it was the only lighted athletic field in the city. The park was demolished in the late 1970s.

Raleigh's largest bus depot, Union Bus Station, was located on West Morgan Street near downtown. A large group of passengers is boarding a motor coach at the depot in 1942.

Fayetteville Street, circa 1942. At left, a recruitment poster for the Marines advertises for enlistees.

Tar Heels supported the war effort in many ways, among them the purchase of war bonds. Stands like this one at Boylan Pearce Department Store sold the bonds, as well as stamps that counted toward the purchase of a bond. Bonds were a means of saving money, but by pulling dollars from circulation, they also reduced inflationary tendencies that accompanied rationing.

East Hargett Street in 1943, where young men of military age are in short supply. As men went overseas to defend the nation in World War II, women and minorities entered the workforce in great numbers to produce the armaments needed in the great conflict.

The 300 block of Salisbury Street, facing north, circa 1943. To the left are the Green Grill, the State Theatre, and other businesses. Century Post Office and Wake County Courthouse are visible on the far right.

The 300 block of Wilmington Street, facing north from Davie Street, in 1943. The rear entrance to the Hudson-Belk Department Store is visible at far-left.

Erected in the early 1940s on the northwest corner of Fayetteville and Davie streets, the Durham Life Insurance Building was briefly Raleigh's tallest structure. Its first floor was home to the S&W Cafeteria, a popular downtown eatery. A neon sign at far-right advertises the Raleigh Diner.

The first swimming pool opened in Raleigh's Pullen Park in 1891. At the time, only male patrons were admitted. By the 1940s, the park boasted a new pool, a popular destination for kids wanting to cool off on a hot summer day.

The east side of the 200 block of Fayetteville Street, 1945. At the Wake Theater, Brad Taylor is starring in *Swingin' on a Rainbow.*

A Golden Tap orange juice truck idles in front of the Garland C. Norris Company building in 1946.

At the conclusion of World War II, Raleigh's Fayetteville Street hosted a joyous parade to honor veterans returning from the war.

Under the neon star at Raleigh's Big Star Mammoth Food Center in 1946, a no. 2 can of fancy peas is selling for 20 cents and a jar of sauerkraut for 17 cents.

Fayetteville Street in 1947. To the left is the neon sign for the Hotel Sir Walter. On the right is the hipped roof of the old Raleigh City Hall.

Homing pigeons take to the air at the Raleigh Seaboard Station in the late 1940s. The pastime of pigeon racing remained popular after the war.

Fayetteville and Hargett
streets, 1947. At center
(left to right) are the
Raleigh Building and the
Odd Fellows Building.

The scene outside the William B. Umstead senatorial campaign headquarters in 1948. Umstead lost the election but would go on to win the governorship of North Carolina in 1952. Governor Umstead died in office in 1954, shortly after appointing a committee to look at the effect of desegregation on North Carolina schools.

"The House That Case Built," Reynolds Coliseum opened on the campus of North Carolina State University in 1949. It became the home court for NCSU's powerhouse basketball squads of the 1950s, coached by the legendary Everett Case.

Evening view of Fayetteville Street in 1949. Hopes were high that postwar prosperity would breathe new life into the state's cities and towns after more than a decade of depression and war.

The main depot for the Seaboard Air Line Railroad as it appeared in 1950.

The city of Raleigh isn't the first settlement in North Carolina bearing that name. From 1584 to 1587 England's Sir Walter Raleigh financed and supplied an expedition from England that landed on the Outer Banks of present-day North Carolina. This endeavor, the first English settlement in the New World, was named Fort Raleigh after the colony's benefactor. It would become known to Americans as the lost colony of Roanoke. In 1950, a re-creation of the fort was built by the National Park Service at Manteo.

An attraction at Fort Raleigh is the outdoor drama "The Lost Colony," performed in this amphitheater. Written by Paul Green, the theatrical production has been enacted each summer since 1937. Fort Raleigh lies some 150 miles east of Raleigh on the Outer Banks.

An aircraft exhibition at Raleigh-Durham Airport circa 1950 brings old and new together as a Marine helicopter rests beside a Wright Brothers–style biplane.

On a day in 1950, E. D. Boney, engineer, and Sam H. Turner, conductor, check their watches beside their Seaboard Railroad diesel locomotive. Despite the growth of trucking firms within the state, the railroads continued to play a vital role in industrial growth across the state and the nation throughout the 1950s.

The opening of Warner Brothers *Bright Leaf* in 1950 is advertised with a parade float. The film, starring Gary Cooper and Lauren Bacall, concerns a tobacco magnate who in 1894 seeks to automate his facilities. In the heart of the Bright Leaf Belt, North Carolinians gave the movie great reviews.

Mr. Peanut presides over the scene at Planters Peanuts on South Wilmington Street, circa 1950s.

This aerial view of the city reveals the changing skyline of the 1950s.

Fayetteville Street remained the center of a bustling mercantile district in the 1950s, but the scene would begin to change in the decades ahead as suburbs and strip malls advanced.

A new Grand Lodge for Raleigh's Freemasons was under construction in the 1950s. These men are examining the cornerstone for the new lodge.

Visible here are the Raleigh Memorial Auditorium in the distance, a historical marker to President Andrew Johnson at lower-left, and various businesses. By the end of the 1960s many of Fayetteville Street's retail merchants were abandoning downtown for new suburban shopping centers and malls.

In 1962, downtown Raleigh was still the place for a stroll during evening hours.

The grounds of the North Carolina State Capitol. The General Assembly moved out of the building in 1962 when the State Legislative Building was completed, but the governor of North Carolina retains an office here. The building's legislative galleries have been restored and are open to the public.

Men are at work on East Davie Street, circa 1964.

Designed by architects Samuel Sloan and A. G. Bauer, the North Carolina Executive Mansion was completed in 1891 on the former Burke Square in Raleigh. The official home for the state's governor and family, the residence is an outstanding example of Queen Anne–style Victorian architecture popular at the end of the nineteenth century.

An aerial view of downtown Raleigh, circa late 1960s. Running up the center of the image is Fayetteville Street, with the State Capitol at its northern terminus and the State Legislative Building just beyond and at the top of the photo.

Notes on the Photographs

These notes, listed by page number, attempt to include all aspects known of the photographs. Each of the photographs is identified by the page number, a title or description, photographer and collection, archive, and call or box number when applicable. Although every attempt was made to collect all data, in some cases complete data may have been unavailable due to the age and condition of some of the photographs and records.

II **Streetcars**
North Carolina State Archives
N.53.15.8932

VI **E. Besson's Tailor Shop**
North Carolina State Archives
N.74.12.483

X **Seaboard Coast Line Building**
North Carolina State Archives
N.77.10.511

2 **Parade**
North Carolina State Archives
N.75.5.448

3 **View of State Capitol**
North Carolina State Archives
N.55.10.16

4 **Raleigh Light Infantry**
North Carolina State Archives
N.79.5.137

5 **Briggs Building**
North Carolina State Archives
N.75.8.354

6 **Yarborough House Hotel**
North Carolina State Archives
N.85.11.17

7 **North Carolina State Capitol**
North Carolina State Archives
N.53.15.353

8 **After the Great Blizzard of 1899**
North Carolina State Archives
N.94.12.36

9 **Digging Out**
North Carolina State Archives
N.63.9.9

10 **Devereux House**
North Carolina State Archives
N.53.15.299

11 **Brantley's Drug Store**
North Carolina State Archives
N.2000.4.25

12 **Eno Station**
Durham County Library
B074

13 **Meredith College**
North Carolina State Archives
N.75.5.396

14 **Nash Square**
North Carolina State Archives
CP&L, f.120

16 **Aunt Betsy**
North Carolina State Archives
N.77.7.68

17 **Fayetteville Street**
North Carolina State Archives
N.69.8.19

18 **Paving East Lane Street, 1906**
North Carolina State Archives
Ph.C.68 CP&L Raleigh
f.188

19 **A Circus Parade**
North Carolina State Archives
N.74.6.565

20 **Family at Falls of the Neuse River**
North Carolina State Archives
N_98_4_38

21 **Citizens National Bank**
North Carolina State Archives
N.53.15.7936

22 **Welcome**
North Carolina State Archives
N.64.8.155

Printed in the USA
CPSIA information can be obtained
at www.ICGtesting.com
JSHW041439270224
58171JS00021B/94